The Magical Adventures of Diesel the Husky

Written and Illustrated by
Perry & Rosie Tobin

First Published in 2023 by Blossom Spring Publishing
The Magical Adventures of Diesel The Husky
Copyright © 2023 Perry and Rosie Tobin

ISBN 978-1-7384130-0-3

E: admin@blossomspringpublishing.com
W: www.blossomspringpublishing.com

All rights reserved under International Copyright Law.
Contents, illustrations and/or cover may not be reproduced in whole or in part without the express written consent of the publisher.
Names, characters, places and incidents are either products of the author's imagination or used fictitiously.

For, Misty, Lizzie, Kaiba, Destiny, Sofia, Izzie, Sami
& Ruby
Our childhood pets,
We miss you everyday.

Once upon a time, in a faraway land covered in snow, there lived a handsome husky named Diesel.

He was known throughout the land for his speed and love of adventure.

Whenever the other dogs heard his howl echoing throughout the snowy hills, they knew he was off on another exciting adventure.

One day, Diesel was racing through the snowy wilderness, when he noticed a strange object sticking out of the snow.

He ran over to investigate and discovered a small, glowing crystal.

As soon as he touched it, he felt a warm energy flowing through his body. Suddenly, the crystal disappeared, and Diesel felt a strange tingling sensation in his paws.

The next thing Diesel knew, he was racing through the snow at lightning speed. He could barely keep up with himself!

He soon realised that the crystal had given him magical powers, allowing him to run faster than he had ever run before.

Over the next few days, Diesel went on all sorts of adventures, racing through the snow, jumping over logs……

and rocks……

And even leaping over frozen rivers. Everywhere he went, he felt the wind in his fur and the thrill of adventure.

Diesel decided to enter a big sledge race in a nearby town.

He had always loved racing, and now that he had his magical powers, he was sure he could win.

As he headed for the starting line, he felt the excitement building inside of him.

As soon as the race started, Diesel took off like a shot.

His sledge glided through the snow, and he felt like he was flying.

He quickly left the others far behind, and soon he was racing alone through the wilderness.

But then, just as he was about to cross the finish line,
Diesel spotted a group of other sledge dogs who had got lost
on the trail.

They were barking for help and Diesel knew he couldn't just leave them behind.

Using his magical powers, Diesel ran back along the trail and found the lost sledge dogs.

He helped them get back on track, and together they all crossed the finish line as the crowd cheered with delight.

From that day on Diesel continued to have magical adventures, but he always remembered the importance of helping others and the thrill of a good race.

And as long as he had his magical powers, he knew there was no adventure he couldn't handle.

To be continued…….

Acknowledgements.

Firstly, we would like to thank our furry companions for being the inspiration behind all of these stories.

Secondly, we would like to thank our children for all of their support and patience whilst creating this series, and being our inspired critics.

Thirdly, we would like to thank our dearest friend Jane, your advice, ideas and your never ending support means more to us than you realise.

And lastly, but certainly not least.
Diesel, you're more than a pet, you're more than a companion, you are our world, and we couldn't love you more if we tried.

About The Author and Illustrator

Perry is from Somerset. He has always struggled with dyslexia but has always been fascinated with books for many years.

Perry dedicates his free time to learning how to read despite his disability. Rosie has helped Perry immensely with reading and understanding the English language. As husband and wife, Perry and Rosie decided to combine their skills of writing and illustrating to creating children's books based on their love for animals, and in particular their pets including their beloved husky Diesel.

Perry and Rosie still live in Somerset with their children and their pets. (five cats and two huskies!)

The Magical Adventures of Diesel the Husky is Perry and Rosie's debut book.

www.blossomspringpublishing.com

www.ingramcontent.com/pod-product-compliance
Lightning Source LLC
Chambersburg PA
CBHW042127040426
42450CB00002B/97